Tradition and Creativity in Japanese Dance

KIKUNOKAI

New York • Weatherhill • Tokyo

Tradition and Creativity in Japanese Dance

KIKUNOKAI

by Michiyo Hata

ACKNOWLEDGMENTS

The author wishes to gratefully acknowledge the contributions of many to the completion of this book, in particular Mr. Hiroshi Mizobuchi, for photography of performances and that appearing in chapter 1, "Dancing in Nature"; Mr. Jin Yoshida, for photography of chapter 2, "The Path," and performances; Kurosawa Production; Kyoto City; Fujieda City, Shizuoka Prefecture; Ashikaga Flower Park, Tochigi Prefecture; Fukumoto, Pontocho, Kyoto; Monju, Gion, Kyoto; and Usui Liquor Shop, Sagano, Kyoto.

Photography: Ezawa Photo Studio, Haruhisa Yamaguchi, Shunichi Takano, and Staff TES; special cooperation and assistance: the Kobayashi family, Nagano Prefecture; Office Kan; Studio Vida; Mr. Takehiro Somei and Mr. Yoshitaka Somei, Somedera, Sekkoji Temple, Nara Prefecture; and Ms. Yoshiko kawamura.

First edition, 2001
© by Michiyo Hata
Published by Weatherhill, Inc.
41 Monroe Turnpike, Tumbull, Connecticut 06611

Protected by copyright under the terms of the International Copyright Union; all rights reserved. Except for fair use in books reviews, no part of this book may be reproduced by any means, including any method of photographic reproduction, without permission of the publisher.

Printed in China.

Library of Congress Cataloging-in-Publication Data available upon request.

Contents

Preface   8

The History of Japanese Dance and Kikunokai   10
  by Haruo Misumi

CHAPTER ONE
Dancing in Nature: The World of Michiyo Hata   12

CHAPTER TWO
Michi—The Way, The Path   38

CHAPTER THREE
Classical Dances   48

CHAPTER FOUR
Kyoto and Kikunokai   62

CHAPTER FIVE
The Works of Kikunokai   102

Chronology   159

The Kikunokai Dance Troupe,

the name of which was derived from chrysanthemums,

was founded by Michiyo Hata in 1972.

Preface

Japan has a rich and ancient cultural heritage, and its artistic legacy is particularly fertile. As one who has devoted her life to dance, I am very proud of this, and I believe it is important to pass on this legacy as well as make new contributions to it. This is my artistic mission.

I founded the dance troupe Kikunokai in 1972 with the aim of bringing the art of Japanese dance from the age of the rigid, classical style of tradition toward a freer and more expansive form of expression that responds to change. I named it after the chrysanthemum, or kiku, a symbol of eternal freshness.

That was almost three decades ago. Now, as we embark on yet another new age, I have written this book to record our work to date, to stimulate our continued growth and innovation, and to make the work and activities of Kikunokai better known throughout the world.

I continue to explore the full range of possibilities in Japanese dance with the constant prayer that dance, the language of the heart, will continue to touch people, to nourish them in spirit, and to engage them in a vibrant dialogue about life and art.

The History of Japanese Dance and Kikunokai

HARUO MISUMI, PRESIDENT, JAPANESE FOLKLORE ASSOCIATION

Dance has a long history in Japan. As in other nations, it began in religious ceremonies.

In ancient rituals, shrine maidens known as *miko* circumambulated the altar holding branches of sacred trees as they summoned and welcomed the gods to the rite. Other ritualists also donned the guise of the gods and acted out the submission of malevolent spirits. These ritual activities were later stylized into dances that were known as Kamiasobi and Kagura.

As these forms of religious dance were flourishing, two continental dance forms, Gigaku and Bugaku, were introduced to Japan from China and Korea in the seventh and eighth centuries and were frequently performed at the imperial court and in temples and shrines. Gigaku quickly disappeared as a living art. Bugaku, in contrast, is a complex and sophisticated art form using wind, string, and percussion instruments and combining elements from India, China, and Central Asia. It went on to have a lasting influence on Japanese dance, and it survives to this day in Japan.

From the ninth through the twelfth centuries, new forms of dance known as Sarugaku and Dengaku were popular in Kyoto. They incorporated mime and acrobatics from the Asian continent into entertainments performed at harvest festivals in farming villages. At around the same time, temple priests developed a performing art based on Bugaku called Ennen. All of these genres contributed to the development of the musical drama known as Noh, which emerged in its present form in the fourteenth century. Noh is a masked drama whose stories are told through dance, mime, song, and chanted dialogue to the accompaniment of flute and three types of drums, the *kotsuzumi, otsuzumi,* and *taiko*. Noh remains one of Japan's important theatrical arts to this day.

While Noh was admired and patronized by the nobility and warrior class, such dance forms as Nembutsu Odori and Furyu Odori were popular among the common people. They were dynamic and rhythmical group dances that consisted mainly of leaping steps. The fifteenth and sixteenth centuries were a period of almost uninterrupted warfare, and the common people, their lives fraught with anxiety and uncertainty, must have found solace in the excitement and community feeling of these group dances.

When the civil wars ended in the early seventeenth century, an itinerant female dancer named Okuni integrated these mass dances with the fashionable customs of the capital city, creating and performing a new genre which was known as Kabuki Odori. Her first "stage" was a dry riverbed in Kyoto, and her performances proved to be exceptionally popular. The word *kabuki is* derived from an obsolete verb, *kabuku,* meaning "to tilt," "to be at the forefront," or "the latest fashion." At its inception, Kabuki Odori was a lively revue-type of entertainment in which female dancers performed boisterously in the most striking and fashionable dress of the day. Women were soon forbidden to appear upon the stage, however, because authorities believed it was an offense against public morality. From the middle of the seventeenth century, only male actors could perform Kabuki, which gradually developed into a combination of drama and dance. With women banned from the stage, men took female roles, and it was from this time that the dances of these female impersonators (*oyama*) were first created. At the same time, dancing techniques became increasingly mimetic, in order to express the meanings of the stories behind the dances. Various costuming and staging devices still employed today also originated at that time.

Kabuki Odori became popular at theatres in Edo (today's Tokyo), Kyoto, and Osaka. Jiuta Mai, on the other hand, developed in the Kyoto-Osaka area as a delicate and elegant chamber dance style, to the accompaniment of a song genre called *jiuta* and the shamisen, a three-stringed banjo-like instrument. The geisha and *maiko* (apprentice geisha) of Gion in Kyoto still perform Jiuta Mai today.

In addition to the above-mentioned dances of the urban centers, farming and fishing villages had many folk dances dating back to ancient times. Though these dances experienced a period of decline in the early modern period, recently their appeal has been recognized anew and several have been revived as performing arts. A number of dancers and choreographers have attempted to creatively adapt and develop these folk dances to make them popular with contemporary audiences.

We are very fortunate to have a dance troupe such as Kikunokai, led by Michiyo Hata, that not only diligently studies the classics but also explores Japan's rich legacy of folk dance. For the past twenty-seven years, this troupe has successfully presented dance-dramas depicting the joys and sorrows of the common people. The troupe is now widely known abroad, as well as in Japan, where it has received the Prize for Outstanding Artistry from the Agency for Cultural Affairs of Japan.

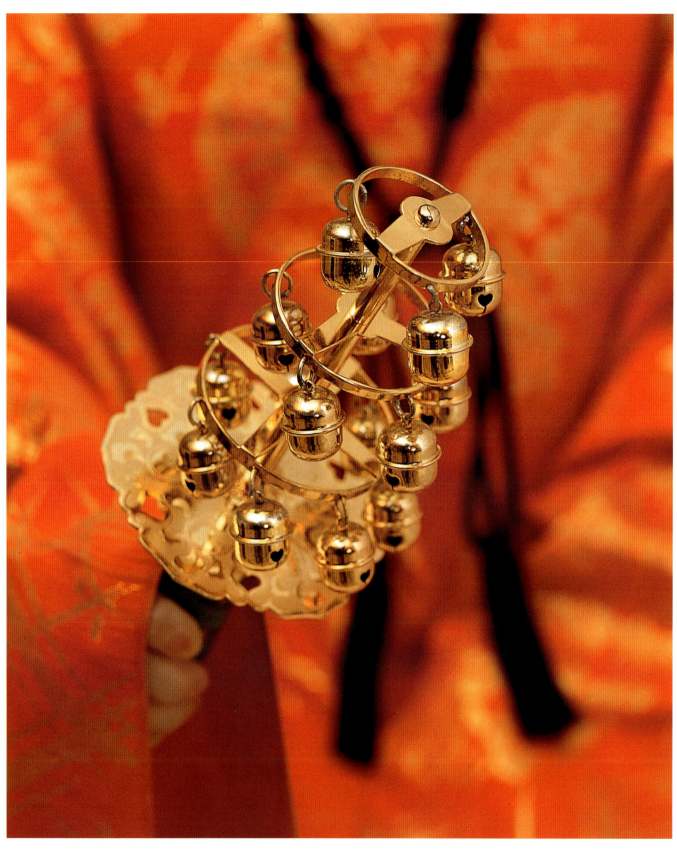

A bell used in a celebratory dance.

Dancing in Nature: The World of Michiyo Hata

CHAPTER ONE

MERGING WITH NATURE

There are many areas of great scenic beauty in Japan. Though I was trained to dance on the boards of the stage, when I encounter one of these scenes I am entranced, and I often feel the desire to make it a different kind of stage where I can dance to my heart's content. My mind fills with images of what color and design of kimono would complement the natural setting, what dance could be performed where, and in what season.

Finally I found the opportunity to perform several of my favorite pieces amidst the flowers, wearing costumes that suited them perfectly. There was no audience; I was alone with nature. Becoming one with the natural setting and performing with a new-found freedom, I savored the dancer's supreme delight: merging with nature.

MUSUME DOJOJI (THE DOJOJI MAIDEN)

Musume Dojoji is one of the classics of the Japanese dance repertoire, with dramatic staging and beautiful costumes. It is based on a legend concerning Dojoji temple in Wakayama Prefecture. A young woman, Kiyohime, falls in love with a handsome young monk, Anchin. She pursues him, but of course he flees, not wishing to break his monastic vows, and hides inside a giant temple bell. The spurned Kiyohime is transformed by her frustration and anger into a giant white snake. She wraps her coils around the bell and melts it, killing herself and her beloved Anchin inside.

Musume Dojoji, performed at Konkai Komyoji temple in Kyoto.

The *kakko* is a percussion instrument used as a dance prop. The drumhead is gilded and it is colorfully decorated with "comma" *(tomoe)* patterns and Chinese peonies and scrolling vines. The *kakko* evolved from a drum used in the ancient musical ensemble imported from China to Japan known as Gagaku, or "elegant music."

The "burning drum" motif, taken from a decorated drum used in Gagaku, depicted on a kimono sleeve. Dragons and clouds surround the central comma motif, and they in turn are enclosed by stylized flames. The most complex and sophisticated techniques of traditional Japanese embroidery are employed to create this beautiful design.

OPPOSITE:
A scene from *Dojoji* performed on the banks of the Kamo River, Kyoto.

The traditional costumes for *Musume Dojoji* all have a cherry-blossom pattern, but the dancer changes seven times, starting with a kimono with a black background, changing to red, blue, pink, purple, yellow, navy blue, and finally white. The costuming is extremely gorgeous, assuming in its brilliance an almost fantastic quality. The embroidered "burning drum" *(kaen daiko)* motif on the yellow kimono shown in the photo is particularly impressive, patiently fashioned by hand, one stitch at a time.

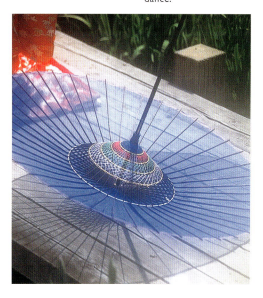

A parasol used in the dance.

AYAME (IRIS)

Japanese iris blooming gloriously in their watery beds alongside the quieter flowers of the sweet rush. Their delicate and shifting shades of lavender, white, purple, and violet penetrate the heart with a mysterious loveliness. The lacquer-red kimono with its palace-scenery motif *(gosho doki)* design stands out brilliantly against the background of the iris reflected in the water, as the dancer is bathed in the overflowing life force of the strong yet subtle green world around her.

Dancing among Japanese irises in Rengeji Park, Fujieda City, Shizuoka Prefecture.

SHIZU NO ODAMAKI (SHIZU'S THREAD WINDING)

Shizuka Gozen, the lover of the tragic warrior hero Minamoto no Yoshitsune, performs this dance in front of Yoshitsune's elder brother Yoritomo. Mistakenly believing that Yoshitsune has betrayed him, Yoritomo has driven him into exile, but Shizuka Gozen is unable to forget her love, and dances and sings with Yoshitsune in her heart. *Odamaki* means to wind thread on a spool. In Japan, lovers are believed to be linked by a red thread from birth; in this dance, Shizu winds that thread.

Shizu no Odamaki, performed at the Ashikaga Flower Park, Ashikaga City, Tochigi Prefecture.

FUJI MUSUME (WISTERIA MAIDEN)

Fuji Musume, or "Wisteria Maiden," is a dance based on a character that was very popular in woodblock prints of the Edo period (1600-1868). The dance is a celebration of female beauty, which is compared to the trailing blossoms of the wisteria in full bloom.

The mysterious figure of the Wisteria Maiden, neither human nor flower, of indeterminate age and even sex, is an ideal subject for dance. It blooms prolifically with a beauty that is unforgettably bewitching. The alluring charm of the wisteria blossom is as fragrant as an endless love.

Fuji Musume, performed at the Ashikaga Flower Park, Ashikaga City, Tochigi Prefecture.

KEISEI

A *keisei* was the highest-ranked courtesan in feudal Japan, not only talented, witty, and sophisticated, but possessing all the charms of a mature woman.

The dance *Keisei*, performed in Rengeji Park, Fujieda City, Shizuoka Prefecture.

Michi—*The Way, The Path*

CHAPTER TWO

How many years have passed since I first began to study Japanese dance? When I look back at the timeless path I have traveled, it seems not long at all. That is the inexhaustible attraction of the Way of Art.

When you are climbing a mountain, the quickest way to the peak is to take the right path. To pursue the Way of Art, one must study the basics with an excellent teacher, practice and perfect oneself in every role, and constantly seek that endless road of artistic mastery.

Let us look at the Way of the Dance, from the beginning, through the eyes of my students.

The first encounter with dance.

RIGHT:
The first time to be dressed in kimono, traditional clothing for classical Japanese dancers.

A new student receives a fan from the teacher to commemorate her entrance into the school and the beginning of her training.

Dance fans.

MICHI — THE WAY, THE ROAD | 41

Traveling to lessons on a rainy day.

Studying the shamisen.

ABOVE
Rehearsing with a dance fan.

FAR LEFT
Practicing the *tsuzumi* hand drum.

LEFT
The hairdresser arranges a young dancer's hair in the traditional style for the first time.

Applying makeup.

Arranging the hair.

BELOW
The flowers of this hair ornament are made from very fine silk pinched into the shape of blossoms. This is an ornament suitable for a young girl wearing a traditional Japanese hairstyle.

Han'eri (half-collar), a strip of cloth that is sewn to the inner collar of the kimono to keep it from getting soiled. One *han'eri* has a ground pattern stitched in platinum thread on the scarlet silk so typical of Kyoto; on the other, a vine pattern is embroidered in white thread. Such *han'eri* are precious and luxurious accessories.

OPPOSITE
Sachiko Tsuruoka learning to wear the costume carefully to keep it from becoming disordered.

Onoe Kikunojo, left, with his mentor Onoe Kikugoro VI.

THE MENTOR

There is nothing more important in our lives than our encounters with others, and especially our encounters with our mentors. The student who is blessed with a mentor of high character and artistic genius is fortunate indeed. My mentor in the art of dance was Onoe Kikunojo I. When he was still a child he became the disciple of the underappreciated Kabuki actor Onoe Kikugoro VI and began his studies to become a Kabuki actor. Onoe Kikugoro VI has been described as one of the most brilliant artists of the Japanese theater.

Japan Broadcasting Corporation announcer Shizuo Yamakawa, in an essay appearing in *Kabuki Kansho Nyumon* (An Introduction to the Enjoyment of Kabuki), recalls, "Honorary Professor of German Literature at Tokyo University, Tomio Tezuka, was once asked in a television interview, 'You are always so modest, but if you were to tell us the thing you were proudest of in your life, what would it be?' Professor Tezuka replied, 'That I saw the actor Onoe Kikugoro VI.' I was astonished. It would never have occurred to me to connect a professor of German literature and a Kabuki actor, especially Kikugoro VI. But after I heard what Professor Tezuka had to say, I understood. 'People tend to think of academic study as something difficult and hard to grasp, but that's wrong. It should be common sense. Literature must be alive. It must have power. And it must, more than anything, be easy to understand. The same is true of Kabuki. Kikugoro VI's theater always has these qualities. In addition, he has the gift to exhibit all of these qualities simultaneously, in a single moment. Having seen him perform is one of the greatest satisfactions of my life.'"

Kikugoro VI was trained by his father, Onoe Kikugoro V, and Ichikawa Danjuro IX, and he performed a wide variety of roles in many different plays, ranging from historical dramas to contemporary works. He was brilliant in male roles, female roles, as young girls, villains, male leads, and character roles, demonstrating a mastery of style and expression that have never been rivaled.

In the traditional world of Kabuki, an actor is rarely allowed to play major roles unless he is born into a long-established acting family. But Onoe Kikugoro VI discovered tremendous dancing talent in my future mentor Onoe Kotojiro, who was not from such a family;

Onoe Kikunojo I.

Kikugoro VI founded a school of dance, the Onoe Ryu (*ryu* means "school"), and made Kotojiro—later to take the name Kikunojo—the central figure of that new school. This was a completely unprecedented development at the time. Kikugoro VI founded the Onoe Ryu in February 1948, selecting Kikunojo from amidst his many students. This was an event of great historical importance in the history of Japanese dance. My mentor Kikunojo's wife said of him, "I can't help but feel tremendous gratitude, respect, and admiration for the large body of fine work he has left as a dancer. He was a man of strong convictions, utterly devoted to his art."

Onoe Kikunojo was extremely strict about lessons, and he was a particularly relentless taskmaster with those seeking to become professional dancers, those who would be dancing before an audience. Studying with him, one was in a constant state of tension, always on the alert. But eventually one came to feel a sense of great satisfaction in a life built around art, and that bracing tension became an indispensable part of one's life.

Onoe Kikugoro VI always used to say that "Art is timing. Timing can become—magic."

I came to understand these words when I danced *Kiku no Izumi* (The Spring of Chrysanthemums) with my mentor Onoe Kikunojo. Both in time and out of time with the music, his marvelous dance had a rhythm all its own. He had already mastered the great truth that dance does not only entail moving in time with the music one hears.

Onoe Kikunojo's final performance was *Kishu Dojoji*, in Hawaii in August 1964. It was at a performance staged by his Hawaiian disciple Onoe Kikunobu, and Kikunojo and I performed. Kikunojo died twelve days later, in Hawaii, at the youthful age of fifty-four.

Even today, when I close my eyes I can see him dancing, sweeping dynamically through space. I am endlessly grateful to him. Without the vigorous training to which he subjected me, I would not be who I am today.

Shakkyo (The Stone Bridge)

Classical Dances

CHAPTER THREE

CLASSICAL JAPANESE DANCE

To become a master of Japanese dance, one must begin by mastering the classic techniques. This includes studying the shamisen, theatrical orchestral music, the chanting style of the puppet theater, and traditional etiquette.

The most widely known form of classical dance is Kabuki dance, but it also includes *kamigata mai,* a dance style born in Kyoto and Osaka.

It is important to remember the obvious fact that what we today know as classical dances, when first performed, were new. The dances that have been passed down to us as classics were loved by their choreographers and dancers, kept alive from generation to generation, and polished and refined until they arrived at their present state of perfection.

Kikunokai places its priority on the study of the classics, and the students train hard every day to practice and perfect them. But we have not restricted ourselves to the classics; we have also created new works. The fundamentals of classical dance are crucial to creating works that will live in a new age; at the same time, the process of creating original works breathes new life into the old favorites.

CHAPTER THREE

OPPOSITE

Suisen Tanzen (Daffodil Jackets). During the Edo period, young samurai and merchants often wore "daffodil jackets" when enjoying themselves in the pleasure quarters. These jackets were designed in bright, flashy colors with daffodil patterns printed or embroidered on the back. *Suisen Tanzen*, based on this popular custom, expresses the gaiety of youth in the Edo period and emphasizes lively dance movements and brilliant costume design.

Kagamijishi (The Lion in the Mirror). In this dance, the shogun requests that the youngest lady-in-waiting perform a celebratory dance. She appears first in her court costume, and she dances with a lion puppet that is resting on the ceremonial alter in the room. Gradually the spirit of the lion enters her body, and in the climactic scene she appears transformed into the lion. This is regarded, along with *Dojoji,* as one of the great works of the classical repertory, and it is renowned for its difficult technique and wide range of expression—from the serving girl, a female role, to the lion, a male role. Only an accomplished dancer would attempt it.

CLASSICAL DANCES | 51

Sagi Musume (Heron Maiden) is the story of a heron who falls in love with a human being and dies for her love. The dancer first appears, thinking of her beloved, in a pure white bridal kimono and headdress. She changes from that to red, then purple, then blue, expressing her passionate love and conflicting feelings. Finally she appears as the white heron, suffering in Hell, her dream of love unfulfilled. The story resembles the famous Western ballet *Swan Lake,* but precedes it by more than a century.

Yasuna tells of the tragic fate of its eponymous hero. Yasuna's lover, Sakaki no Mae, is forced into prostitution and kills herself. Yasuna goes mad with grief, and carrying one of Sakaki no Mae's robes he wanders into a spring field ablaze with brilliant yellow mustard blossoms. It is a dance expressing the deep sorrow of a young man.

OPPOSITE:

Kasane is a ghastly tale of love gone mad. The male lead, Yoemon (here played by Onoe Kikugoro VII), has killed a man. He and the beautiful Kasane fall in love, neither realizing that Yoemon's victim was Kasane's father. The father's skull washes ashore and places a curse on Kasane, making Yoemon deeply aware of his sin. Kasane is gradually transformed into an ugly hag with a huge wound across her face, exactly like the wound Yoemon inflicted on her father's face with a sickle. Yoemon kills Kasane and is in turn destroyed by her ghost.

Yoemon: Kikugoro Onoe VII
Kasane: Kikunori Onoe (Michiyo Hata)

The text of the dance *Kishu Dojoji* (Dojoji in Ki Province) is the closest version of *Dojoji* to that of the Noh play *Dojoji*, and the costuming is also similar to the Noh costume. The dance, however, was choreographed by Kabuki actors.

OPPOSITE
Kane no Misaki (The Cape of the Bell) is almost identical to *Musume Dojoji*, except in this version a high-ranking courtesan pursues the man she loves.

CLASSICAL DANCES

OPPOSITE

In *Aki no Irokusa* (The Bright-hued Autumn Grasses), the lord of the Nambu fief gives the great singer Kineya Rokuzaemon (here played by the third Iemoto of the Onoe Ryu, Onoe Kikunojo II) a difficult text filled with Chinese words to set to music, hoping to discredit him. Rokuzaemon, however, succeeds in setting the words beautifully. This is a dreamlike dance that acts out the beautiful autumn scenes described in the lyrics.

Man: Kikunojo Onoe II
Woman: Kikunori Onoe (Michiyo Hata)

Shinkyoku Urashima (The New Seas and Islands) was written by Tsubouchi Shoyo, a writer and translator of Shakespeare into Japanese in the second half of the 1800s. It describes the changing faces of the sea through the four seasons.

Michiyo Hata

Matsukaze is based on a Noh play and, in the Kabuki version, tells the story of Matsukaze, a young woman, a salt-gatherer by profession, who is abandoned by her lover and goes mad with grief. It is a sad and haunting work.

LEFT AND OPPOSITE
Osen is the story of the beauty Osen, who worked at a tea shop in the precincts of Kasamori Shrine, and her lover, a popular Kabuki actor of the day. It is a sweet tale based on prints of the great woodblock artist Suzuki Harunobu.

Kyoto and Kikunokai

CHAPTER FOUR

MY KYOTO

Whenever I am asked when the history of dance began, I reply, "From the day people appeared on earth."

I was born in Kyoto, the cradle of Japanese culture, and I still spend a great deal of time there. I am glad that I was born there because the four seasons are so distinct in Kyoto. Dance is intimately linked to the changes in the natural world through the year, and living in Kyoto cultivated in me a heightened sensitivity to what we describe in Japan as "the flowers, birds, wind, and moon" or "the snow, the moon, the flowers."

I still remember the huge snowflakes—we call them "peony snowflakes"—that fall in the winter. Icicles sharp as daggers hanging from the eaves. The mysterious color of the crescent moon. The way the buds of the cherry tree, patiently conserving their strength through the winter, transform themselves with the warm days of spring. When the blossom-filled spring arrives, butterflies dance, the breezes invite, and the moon is shaded with mist.

It is hard to brag about the oppressive heat of summer in Kyoto, but I remember enjoying wonderful moments of cool in the shade of the bamboo blinds that hung down

from the eaves of our house. Willow trees grow along the river, and fireflies dance among their leaves. Even after dusk had fallen, the cicadas continued to drone sweetly in the trees behind the house.

I recall the beauty of the leaves in autumn, transformed from green to scarlet by the cold of a single night.

I wake up one morning and frost is on the ground. Dipping my hands in the wooden bucket to wash my face in the morning, I break the thin skin of ice and a keen flash of cold runs through my body. I slide open the doors to the garden and encounter nature's beauty close at hand.

I cannot begin to measure the degree to which the changes of the four seasons have enriched my life. The seasons are overflowing with the vibrancy of life.

I have danced through these beautiful seasons from the day I was born. I dance continuously, even in my dreams. There is a part of me that can lift its wings as freely as a gull, and soar dancing into the skies. I dance to music or even without music, but always to a wonderful sound that pours out from my innermost being. At those times, even the rays of light that penetrate the thin silk of my kimono seem to change and shift from moment to moment.

Time passes, the seasons change. The four seasons of our lives, too, should begin and end with cherry blossoms. I hope to express truth through the medium of dance because this is linked to the power that wells up within us and causes us to dance. Dance is the art of the moment in which the joy of being alive has been transmitted from ancient times.

Whether dancing on the boards of a stage or on bare earth, it is always my wish to express my feeling freely, without inhibitions. I want to keep on dancing, shining with the overflowing beauty of all being, and express the eager vibrancy of all life.

The Four Seasons of Kyoto

OPPOSITE
Spring: A weeping cherry tree, famous for the beauty of its blossoms, in Maruyama Park.

Summer: The lush greenery of the cedars of Kitayama.

ABOVE
Winter: Snow in the garden of Tofukuji temple.

Autumn: Autumn colors at Togetsukyo Bridge, Arashiyama.

The Kamo River.

The Kamo River is one of Kyoto's main rivers. Kyoto's Kabuki theater, the Minamiza, is located just across the Shijo Avenue Bridge spanning the river. In December of each year, a star-studded performance called *kaomise*, or "face-showing," is held at the Minamiza. This hair ornament with little white pompoms is called a *mochibana kanzashi*, and is worn by apprentice geisha, or *maiko*, in December. Autographs of the *maiko's* favorite actors are written on the *kanzashi*.

The black silk kimono with a crest is the most formal costume of the *maiko*. During the New Year holiday, *maiko* visit their neighbors and pay a formal greeting. The hair ornament worn during the New Year is always a rice stalk. The crested shop curtain hanging in front of establishments where *maiko* reside is also a special New Year decoration. Kyoto preserves the traditional customs of old Japan to this day.

A young geisha, or *maiko*.

A *mochibana kanzashi*.

The Kyoto Minamiza.

Pontocho, an area with many geisha houses, near the Kamo River.

Kikunokai's Yase Training Center is near the Kyoto International Conference Center, by Takaragaike at the foot of Mount Hiei. Yase is famous for its beautiful scenery, preserving the flavor of old Kyoto.

Takanogawa, seen from the training center.

The Yase Training Center.

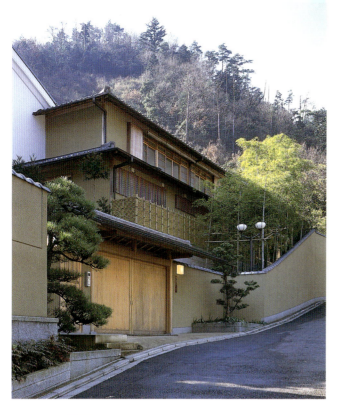

LEFT, ABOVE
The gateway to the Yase Training Center.

LEFT
The entrance way interior.

RIGHT, ABOVE
A stone stairway ascending through a bamboo grove.

RIGHT, BELOW
A specially crafted roof tile with a chrysanthemum crest.

LEFT
The garden seen from the south.

The reception room.

Detail of the mother-of-pearl inlaid doors in the reception room.

The shell used for creating the different mother-of-pearl motifs.

The mother-of-pearl-inlaid doors in the reception room of the Yase Training Center employ the most advanced techniques of the art of lacquerware. There are four door panels, each 2 meters high and 1.18 meters wide. Decorated with chrysanthemums and a vine motif in mother-of-pearl, the doors are very rare and precious. The lacquer is polished to a mirror shine with, in the final stages, the palm and fingertips. The work was done by the Keizuka Lacquerware Workshop. Artist Yunen Nomura used over seven hundred shells to create the mother-of-pearl design.

The curtain for studio performances is the traditional heavy tapestry curtain called a *doncho* in Japanese. A large number of flowers are shown blooming around a pine tree, expressing the hope that many fine dancers will come forth from Kikunokai. The curtain was woven in the Nishijin district of Kyoto, the center of traditional high-quality Japanese textile production, by Tatsumura Art Weavers. Because once the curtain goes up the stage will be filled with bright colorful costumes, the curtain is woven in quiet colors against a gold background.

Large room.

The stage curtain, entitled *Shoju Senso no Mai* (Dance of Venerable Pine and Wild Flowers), a genuine Nishijin brocade woven by the Tatsumura Art Weavers.

ABOVE
The pine tree painted on the back of the stage is taken from the Noh theater. It is used when dances based on the comic Noh interludes called *kyogen* or other celebratory dances are performed. The ceremony to dedicate the opening of the Yase Training Center began on a stage with this pine-tree background.

LEFT
Guests on the opening day of the Yase Training Center.

OPPOSITE, ABOVE
Kotobuki Kiku Sambaso is a dance originating in a celebratory Noh play. It is performed as a prayer for peace and good harvests, and was featured at the opening of the Yase Training Center.

BELOW
A rehearsal studio at the Training Center.

Fuji Musume (Wisteria Maiden). The beauty and drama of this work have made it a perennial favorite. Though best known as a solo work, it also exists in ensemble versions, as shown here.

Nobuko Watanabe
Mika Nakamura
Sachiko Tsuruoka
Yuko Aoki
Yasuko Inoshita

interior.

RIGHT, ABOVE
A stone stairway ascending through a bamboo grove.

RIGHT, BELOW
A specially crafted roof tile with a chry-santhemum crest.

LEFT

Shakkyo (The Stone Bridge). A Buddhist monk arrives at Kongozan in China and finds a small bridge. A mysterious child suddenly appears and tells him not to dare to cross it. The child then transforms into a lion and dances vigorously.

White Lions: Eiji Iida, Norio Takei
Red Lions: Nagamitsu Satake, Hideharu Takeda, Akio Tomidokoro

Nagare means "flow." This work is performed to a shamisen solo. It begins by depicting the single drops of water quietly falling high in the mountains, until they join into a mountain stream, then a river that flows to the sea. The composer is likening the flow of the history of art to the rushing flow of life.

Yuki Shinshin (The Soft Sound of Falling Snow) is a popular Japanese song. This dance, set to that song, depicts the complicated feelings of a man and woman in love.

Man: Eiji Iida
Woman: Yuko Aoki

OPPOSITE:
Shishi no Jidai means "Age of Lions." This dance depicts strong young men living in an age of war.

Yasushige Tsuruoka
Norio Takei
Akio Tomidokoro

82 | CHAPTER FOUR

OPPOSITE:
Soshunfu (Symphony of Youth) depicts another hallowed theme, the celebration of spring by young people. It is set to a famous song of the same name that has been a favorite in Japan since the first decades of the last century.

Yozakura Oshichi, or "Oshichi and the Cherry Blossoms at Night," is an ensemble work depicting the complex feelings of a woman in love.

Teruko Nakayama
Yuko Aoki

Kawa no Nagare no Yo ni (Like a Flowing River) is an ensemble work for a large group of women, featuring the flowing movements of a river.

OPPOSITE:
Hana no Ran, or "A Turmoil of Flowers," is the tragic love story of a man and wife, set in Japan's warring medieval period.

Man: Shigeru Edaki
Wife: Nobuko Watanabe

OPPOSITE
Utamaro depicts the shifting thoughts of women who haven't lost their spiritual purity in spite of their lowly profession.

Echizen Takemai (The Bamboo Dance of Echizen) likens the faithfulness of a woman to a straight bamboo stalk.

Chiru Sakura (Falling Cherry Blossoms) depicts a mighty warrior fighting bravely in Japan's medieval wars, likening his brief moment of glory to the cherry blossoms, which bloom brilliantly but scatter quickly.

Warrior: Michiyo Hata

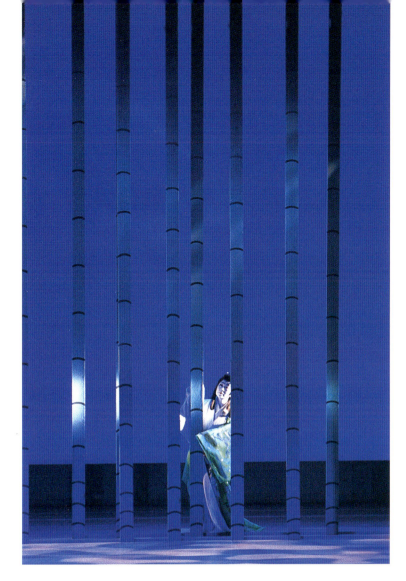

Otome Dake (Bamboo Maiden). An allegorical fantasy about a young "bamboo spirit" who longs to free herself from the rigid constraints of her bamboo existence and yearns for the larger outside world. She fights tenaciously against the laws that govern the bamboo world, but they are too strong for her and she collapses, exhausted, only to discover in a ray of moonlight falling on the bamboo grove a heretofore unseen path to a new life.

JAPANESE HUMOR

I had a very interesting experience once when we were giving a performance at an elementary school in France. We were presenting Tsuri Onna *(Fishing for Wives), a humorous piece in which a feudal lord and his servant each fish for a wife. The lord pulls up a beauty, but the servant pulls up an ugly mate. The servant slowly pulls off the beautiful gown the ugly woman is hiding under, revealing her frightening face. Just then, a low chuckle, like the sophisticated laughter of adults, swept through the audience. Later someone who had seen the performance said to me, "I had no idea the Japanese had such a sense of humor!" But humor is a very important, even ubiquitous, element in Japanese culture, and in many of our pieces we present this unique brand of comedy, burnished over the centuries, that is largely unknown outside Japan.*

Migawari Zazen (Substitute for Zazen) is based on a comic Noh interlude, or *kyogen*. The lord wants to pay a visit to his mistress Hanago, and to deceive his wife he tells her he is practicing Zen meditation. He seats his trusty servant in the Zen position and covers him with a robe, then leaves. His wife, of course, finds out, and obtains her comic revenge.

Written by Shiko Okamura
Choreography by Kikunojo Onoe I
Music by Mitaro Kineya

Ukyo Yamakage (Lord): Yasushige Tsuruoka
Tamanoi (Wife): Satoshi Hara
Tarokaja (Servant): Nagamitsu Satake

In *Tsuri Onna* (Fishing for Wives), a lord and his servant, Tarokaja, both of whom are bachelors, have been praying that they will each find the perfect woman. While they sleep, the gods send each a vision of his future wife. The lord fishes up a beauty, and the servant fishes up an ugly woman. The choreography of this piece is based on the *kyogen* piece of the same name. There is also a beloved Kabuki version.

Written by Mokuami Kawatake
Choreography by Kikunojo Onoe I
Music by Shikisa Kishizawa VI

Daimyo (Lord):
Shigeru Edaki
Beautiful Woman:
Yuko Aoki
Tarokaja (Servant):
Satoshi Hara
Ugly Woman:
Nagamitsu Satake

Hanakaja is the name of a petty thief who breaks into a house and inadvertently causes a raucous quarrel between the husband and wife who live there.

Written and directed by Masao Sugi
Choreography by Michiyo Hata
Music by Eizaburo Kineya
Set design by Shigeru Nagakura

Thief: Satoshi Hara
Master: Yasushige Tsuruoka
Wife: Nagamitsu Satake

Memories of Akira Kurosawa

I only knew Akira Kurosawa for a short time, but in that brief interval he taught me a great deal and has left me with memories that are as fresh and inspiring as a scene from one of his films. I choreographed his film *Dreams* and members of Kikunokai performed in the film. I am very grateful for that experience, which allowed me to come into direct contact with his enormous talent and learn many things from a world-renowned master of film.

When I was first contacted by Mr. Kurosawa's staff, I was certain that I could not do what they were asking, and I refused then and there. They called me again, however, and I decided to at least go and meet Mr. Kurosawa.

At that first encounter, I was impressed by his large physical stature and his quiet, steady gaze. He had a remarkable aura of composure and serenity. I asked him to please fire me if he wasn't satisfied with my work, and he said kindly, "I'm sure we can work it out together." He then passed me a file of drawings that he had made recording his ideas for the images he wanted. A wonderful imaginary world was recorded in those pictures in a very accessible form.

My teacher Onoe Kikunojo used to stress how important it was that students share the same understanding as their teacher, so I was very grateful that Mr. Kurosawa had provided me with these concrete images to work from. I was also surprised to see how carefully and clearly he prepared the scenes. Those pictures are one of my great treasures today.

We spent a long time deciding on the make-up for the film's first episode, "The Foxes' Wedding." Though it seemed to go on forever, I was impressed by Mr. Kurosawa's way of working, leading us to the perfect solution through patient and detailed instructions, and also by his keen powers of discernment.

"The Foxes' Wedding," is based on a dream Mr. Kurosawa had when he was five years old.

In Japan there is a folk belief that foxes hold their weddings, forming a procession to escort the bride to her new home, on days when the sun shines through the rain. The mother in this episode tells her son, "The foxes do not like to be seen by people, so even if you chance upon such a wedding procession, you must not look." One day, however, the boy sees just such a wedding procession passing through a grove of cedars. The foxes sense that the boy has seen them and look back at him with a terrifying expression. The frightened child rushes away, but when he gets back home his mother is waiting for him at the front gate, an angry expression on her face. "The foxes came here, and

they were very angry. They said you must commit suicide to make amends. You had better go find them and throw yourself on their mercy and ask for forgiveness, even if you don't return alive. The foxes' home is underneath the rainbow. You can't come home again unless they forgive you." The boy goes off, walking through a field of flowers, heading for the foxes' home beneath the rainbow, and there the dream ends.

Looking at the sketches of the foxes' wedding procession and listening to the music Mr. Kurosawa sent me, I almost immediately came up with the choreography. At last the day when I would show it to Mr. Kurosawa at his studio in Yokohama arrived. The dancers were waiting in a corner of the studio. Mr. Kurosawa gave the cue to start, and as soon as it was finished he said, "The first two movements are good, but for the third, use that pose where they stoop a little and then look ahead, alert for danger. And then do this and then do that . . ." giving very detailed instructions for changes. Then he went on, "All right, just as I said now, let's start again!"

Thinking, "My, we're going full steam ahead!" I rushed back to the dancers and spent thirty seconds or so confirming the director's revisions. The procession began again, but several dancers at the rear of the procession hadn't been able to hear either Mr. Kurosawa or my instructions

The process of filming *Yume* (Dream).

clearly, and Mr. Kurosawa immediately called out in a loud voice, "Some of you are out of step!" The blocking of the scene was completed at this very fast pace.

Though the atmosphere was tense, Mr. Kurosawa always expressed his wishes clearly and the performers understood and accepted his instructions. Mr. Kurosawa was considerate and encouraging throughout, and we began our rehearsals in earnest. I wanted them all to be

The first story: "The Foxes' Wedding."

so well prepared that we would complete the scene on the first take.

The scene was filmed at the cedar grove of Asama Shrine, in Fuji Yoshida City, Yamanashi Prefecture. Makeup began before dawn, and it was very funny to see the dancers jumping in astonishment as they saw another actor in the eerie fox makeup creeping down the dim hallways of the shrine.

When filming was ready to start, a heavy cloud appeared over the forest and sat there, preventing us from shooting. While we were waiting for light, the dancers' feet grew so cold that they were losing feeling in them, so a bonfire was built for them to warm themselves. With the fox mouthpieces on, they couldn't open their mouths, so we broke cookies into little pieces and fed them a crumb at a time as we waited.

At about 4:00 in the afternoon, even Mr. Kurosawa was losing patience, and he suggested we take a break. The dancers realized that he was only saying that out of concern for them, and not one of them moved. If they took a break now, they knew there would be no further shooting that day. When he saw them all standing there waiting patiently, Mr. Kurosawa shouted, "All right! One more time!" and shooting began. It ended at 4:50, and the dancers hadn't had anything substantial to eat all day.

Mr. Kurosawa was very good at discovering and nurturing talent. I also think that the team he built throughout his career had a unity and cohesiveness I have never seen elsewhere. My memories of that time still come back to me as if it were yesterday.

The second story, "Peach Garden," was a dream about the doll festival. A young boy brings sweets to his sister and her friends who are celebrating the doll festival. There were supposed to be just enough sweets for each of the girls, but when handing them out he realizes that there is one extra sweet. Puzzled, he looks out into the garden and sees a strange little girl—the spirit of the peach trees—looking back at him. He chases after her, and finds himself in a terraced field of peach trees behind the house, where a large group (sixty in all) of life-size dolls are stand-

The fox makeup.

ing, dressed in their gorgeous court robes. The dolls say, "We won't ever visit your house again. Your family have cut down all the peach trees. The fallen peach trees are weeping." But one of the princess dolls defends him, saying, "No, this is the good boy, the one who cried when they cut down the trees." The other dolls, having learned the truth, perform a wonderful dance for the boy. When the dance is over they disappear, and all that remain are the sad stumps of the trees.

Mr. Kurosawa wanted the actors' faces to look like actual *hina* dolls, so the main selection of the actors was based mainly on this physical resemblance. Most of the actors chosen were from the *Nijuki-kai*, Kurosawa's cherished team of twenty people who appear in all of his movies. Some of the cast, therefore, had no dancing experience at all, and we held a month of intensive lessons for them.

This turned out to be effective, and the day of the shooting went smoothly, finishing up at about 1:00 in the afternoon. The location was a hillside in Kirigaoka, Midori Ward, Yokohama. It had been rented the year before, cut into layered terraces like the stand used to display the dolls, and grass was planted over it. We came back six months later, and cameras were set up on the opposing bank, facing the hill.

It rained the day before shooting, and I watched anxiously as the actors climbed to their places, holding their long trailing scarlet robes, praying that they would not muddy their costumes.

The actors were concentrating so strongly that they may not have noticed it, but the final scenes, when a blizzard of peach blossoms rains down, was so beautiful that it seemed otherworldly. I will never forget that scene, as several cranes dumped huge quantities of peach petals all at once; it was like, truly, a dream. I repeated "Thank you, thank you" over and over again in my heart, filled with gratitude that Mr. Kurosawa had granted me the privilege of experiencing this moment.

I picked up some of the blossoms and there were many different colors—nearly white pink, pale pink, medium pink, and deep pink—and different sizes, too, so that they fell so beautifully and naturally.

The eighth dream was "Village with a Water Wheel." It is set in a picturesque village, green with trees and featuring an old water wheel. A young man is talking to an old man who says he is one hundred three years old. "We have no electricity or machines to plow our fields. The villagers want to preserve the old way of life as

ABOVE
The Japanese dolls come to life in the second story, "Peach Garden."

RIGHT
Akira Kurosawa and Michiyo Hata observing the filming.

much as possible. People are a part of nature. Nature is the most important thing to us, but when we destroy and pollute it, the polluted air and water pollute human hearts," he says.

Just then cries of rejoicing are heard. "Is it a festival?" asks the young man. "It's a funeral," says the old man. "She lived well, she worked hard, and now we're saying 'You did well' and celebrating her. We don't have any temples in this village, so we see her off to the graveyard ourselves." The old man takes a bell and a branch of flowers and joins the funeral parade. The young man leaves, having learned something important from the old man and the wonderful village.

We had spent a month teaching the actors playing dolls to dance, so we didn't have much time for this funeral procession. I hoped to finish it in one day.

The village, built near a *wasabi* farm in Hodaka-cho, Minami Azumi County, Nagano Prefecture, was a realization of an ideal village Mr. Kurosawa had always envisioned. Construction began several months before shooting; it was a wonderful place, a place you'd like to live in for the rest of your life. Walking along the river bank, I noticed several people wearing aqualungs swimming in the river. I wondered what on earth they were doing, and only later learned that they were making the gracefully floating water plants in the river, attaching them one at a time to the river banks and bottom. This scene was to appear at the end of the film, behind the credits.

Mr. Kurosawa called me close and said, "The old man will break a branch off from a tree in the garden and then take the lead in the old woman's funeral procession, dancing as he goes toward the graveyard. Please choreograph that dance." It didn't seem like I should ask a lot of questions; I came up with just one, to clarify his intent: "Sambaso, right?" I was relieved when he answered, "That's right. That will be perfect."

The funeral procession in the eighth story, "Village with a Water Wheel."

At eighty-five, Chishu Ryu was eighteen years younger than the one hundred and three year old man he played. He had many lines, and he remembered them all perfectly, but he had a harder time with choreography. I devised movements that would be easy for him to remember and perform, and had him repeat them over and over.

He was a hard worker, and he kept practicing even during breaks. He performed wonderfully during the shooting. He was so good that I hoped that I could do as well at his age. I thought that Mr. Kurosawa must be extremely pleased with this last scene.

The press conference on the set after we finished filming was very pleasant and went on for some time. I later heard that press conferences were usually over rather quickly, but this one went on so long that the crew members turning the water wheel by hand were exhausted.

After finishing filming the three segments that I had choreographed, Mr. Kurosawa said a warm and sincere "Thank you" to me.

When I heard that Mr. Kurosawa had died, a shock raced through my heart. Sensing that he would not have liked formal mourning, I attended

his wake wearing a black crested kimono. The funeral was already over, and his staff was all gathered, just as if they were preparing to shoot another film. His son Hisao, president of Kurosawa Productions, gave a little speech.

"Thank you all for coming," he began. "Seeing you all here makes me realize what wonderful friends and colleagues my father has left behind. Thank you all, from the bottom of my heart."

All those who have worked with Mr. Kurosawa were, I am certain, drawn to his utter devotion to his art and will continue to feel his presence as long as they live.

ABOVE, LEFT
Working on choreography with actor Chishu Ryu.

ABOVE
Akira Kurosawa.

The Works of Kikunokai

CHAPTER FIVE

The roots of the traditional arts run very deep in Kyoto, the city of my birth, and all of Japan's performing arts have a long history and strong base there; they are so well understood that words are not even needed to describe them. Naturally, such a degree of perfection and maturity in the arts of the Kyoto-Osaka area also leads to a desire for new forms, and new and old exist together in Kyoto. Growing up in this environment, my first trip to Tokyo when I was fourteen years old was quite a shock.

Kyoto's refined, ancient manner and Tokyo's freshness and vigor; Kyoto's gorgeous and elaborate kimonos, so heavy that we sometimes joke about being "buried" in them, and Tokyo's almost over-simplified style of dress, energized with the spirit of urban chic: over the years I have aimed to absorb the best of both worlds, the products of their differing histories and attitudes toward life.

One of the things that all classical dancers are warned against is watching folk dances or listening to folk music. The classical and folk arts are of course very different. They have developed in different circumstances and have had different aesthetic aims. The world of classical dance has always insisted that there should be no contact with the folk tradition. I was raised and trained in that tradition, but I had an experience that utterly transformed my way of thinking and eventually led to founding Kikunokai in 1972.

It happened when the well-known ethnologist Haruo Misumi asked me to work on a project for the Osaka World Expo, in 1970. I began a trip all around Japan to observe traditional dances so that we could choreograph a sort of folk-dance anthology for the expo. As I visited different localities, my preconceived notions about the folk tradition were uprooted and completely overturned. Here were the stories of the farmers and fishermen who had weathered harsh climates and survived hard times to feed Japan. The dances and songs that had sustained them through all this had so much more power and real human energy than the classical arts, sheltered by tradition and privilege. Though the actual dance techniques of the folk arts may be less polished, the very real joys and sorrows of harvests rich and poor had given these people and their arts a living reality that communicates directly to the viewer. This experience helped me awaken anew to the wonder and power of the human spirit.

It also convinced me of the worth of presenting not only classical dance but also substantive and challenging performances of folk dance and music on the stage, and we have worked hard and long to achieve this goal. In my travels I learned that the folk art

of each region is firmly rooted in the life of that local area, and it changes as one moves from south to north in both form and tempo, reflecting and at the same time preserving the forms and tempos of local life. I wanted to create dances based on these local motifs and modes. I requested the assistance of Mr. Misumi, and from that collaboration, several works in a new "dance-drama" form were born. One of those works won the Prize for Outstanding Artistry at the Cultural Festival sponsored by the Agency for Cultural Affairs of Japan.

At the same time, I have continued to create more personal works harking back to the classical tradition throughout my career. I find this dual approach both stimulating and necessary to my growth as a dancer and choreographer.

106 | CHAPTER FIVE

KANBOTAN
(Winter Peony)

The winter peony withstands the cold winds and snow to bloom in the midst of winter. This work depicts the noble beauty of this flower and a life lived in its mold.

Written by Haruo Misumi
Choreography by Michiyo Hata
Music by Toshimitsu Tanaka

Dancer: Michiyo Hata

MIKO NO TSUKA
(The Prince's Burial Mound)

Miko no Tsuka tells the story of Prince Otsu, the second son of Emperor Temmu. A youth of great promise, he was murdered by political rivals. Just before he was killed, he glanced at a beautiful woman. Unable to find rest because of this vision, the spirit of the prince arises from his burial mound and calls out to the woman. She comes, and they dance together, finally entering a fantasy world in which they are united in an otherworldly love.

Directed by Shigeru Yokoi
Choreography by Michiyo Hata
Music by Nao Yamamoto

Prince Otsu: Michiyo Hata

IZUTSU
(The Well Curb)

Written by Katsuichiro Kaiza
Directed by Shigeru Yokoi
Music by Gosakichi Kineya
Costume design by Hiroshi Hori

Izutsu (The Well Curb), based on a Noh play by Zeami, is a story of a woman's heartsickness for lost love. A young boy and girl fall in love while gazing at their reflections in the bottom of a well. In later years the man marries another, and the woman pines for him, donning a man's robe and gazing longingly down into the well's depths.

SHIROI TORI
(White Bird)

Directed by Shigeru Yokoi
Choreography by Michiyo Hata
Music by Nao Yamamoto

Shiroi Tori (White Bird) is an allegory likening the hard road to becoming a true dance artist to a single white bird soaring into the bitterly cold winter sky.

HANAORE TOGE
(Hanaore Pass)

Directed by Shigeru Yokoi
Choreography by Michiyo Hata
Music by Teizo Matsumura
Set design by Hisanori Fujimoto

Hanaore Toge (Hanaore Pass) is a dance describing the life of Setsuko Mitsuhashi, a female painter who struggled against disease and yet devoted her short life to the creation of beautiful art. It expresses her joy in life and the strength of spirit she demonstrated in challenging her harsh destiny.

THE WORKS OF KIKUNOKAI

OKUNI KABUKI AND THE MINAMIZA

The historic Minamiza is located at the eastern end of the Shijo Bridge in central Kyoto. It is one of the few theaters in Japan equipped for Kabuki performances, along with the Kabukiza theaters in Osaka and Tokyo, and the Shimbashi Embujo, also in Tokyo. The Minamiza is relatively small, but the December *kaomise* performance—an all-star bill featuring the actors who will appear at the theater in the following year—is an important performance for any Kabuki actor.

A stone marker in front of the Minamiza commemorates it as the site of the origin of Kabuki. Historical records tell us that the founder of Kabuki, Izumo no Okuni, performed in the 1600s very near here, on the banks of the Kamo River at Shijo-gawara, Gojo-gawara, and Kitano Temmangu Shrine. My first stage performance was on the boards of the Minamiza. Since moving to Tokyo, it was always my wish to dance the life of Okuni at the Minamiza.

In August 1995 I realized my ambition. It became one of Kikunokai's largest-scale works. The story begins with a leap in time back to 1603, where it unfolds and then jumps back to the present. It includes eight complete changes of costume, in which the costume, wig, and makeup have to be changed within four minutes. Many of my former students are now geisha, and they came to see the performance, bringing their fellow geisha and apprentice geisha.

Mr. Misumi wrote the following passage for the program: "At last *Okuni Kabuki*, which Michiyo Hata asked me to write two years ago, is completed. But the idea of the piece was there from the very beginning. As the dancer Michiyo Hata thinks of Izumo no Okuni, her spirit slips back to Okuni's time and she relives the experiences of Okuni's life.

"Of course, we know little about Okuni, including even her dates of birth and death. All we have are tantalizing fragments: when she was still a girl, during the last years of the sixteenth century, she traveled around Japan performing *yayako odori*, a dance of young children; she later married a performer of comic interludes *(kyogen)* by the name of Sanjuro; she may have had an affair with the eccentric dandy and artist Nagoya Sanzaburo; she went on to create the new genre of Kabuki dance and was a very popular performer; and then at some point she turned over her troupe to her successor and disappeared.

"Knowing so little of Okuni's life, how could Hata revisit scenes from it? I decided that the only approach was for Hata, as a fellow artist, to apprehend the artistic spirit or essence that we can sense emanating from those scraps of Okuni's life story, and make that the main focus

of the drama. What was that spirit? To put one's whole life and being into the dance. To dance as if it were one's last moment. From the days when she was performing *yayako odori*, Okuni danced in a different place, before a different audience, each day, giving herself entirely to each performance and then going on to dance with the same spirit the next day. That ability to dance with utter freshness every day, in a new place, before a new audience, eventually grew into Okuni's creation of what we call Kabuki dance, a new form that discarded all past conventions. Of course she did not do this alone, and I chose the character Nagoya Sanzaburo to represent those who helped her achieve this. He was a genuine rebel, a person for whom there was no past or future, a person who threw everything—all his wealth, his energy, his affections—into the present moment. He lived without regrets. His passion merged with that of Okuni, creating an aesthetic realm of spontaneous creativity: "Let's be revolutionary!" After that brilliant moment, he went on with his life, tossing aside as a spent dream the Kabuki he had helped to create. It was with these thoughts

in mind that I finally finished the script and presented it to Hata."

I looked forward to the performance at the Minamiza, which so many had helped become a reality, in the spirit of dancing here and now, as if this one moment were my entire life.

THE WORKS OF KIKUNOKAI | 113

OKUNI
KABUKI

Written and directed by
Haruo Misumi
Choreography by
Michiyo Hata
Music by Toshimitsu
Tanaka
Set and costume design
by Yusuke Misumi

Okuni, the creator of Kabuki, performs in Kyoto, to which she has come from her home in Izumo.

Okuni's troupe performs in Kyoto, where they attain great popularity.

Okuni meets Nagoya Sanza, and they dance together.

Okuni: Michiyo Hata
Nagoya Sanza: Tokusaburo Arashi

Okuni's troupe during a Kyoto festival.

THE WORKS OF KIKUNOKAI | 115

Okuni ponders her parting, over artistic differences, with Nagoya Sanza.

Okuni: Michiyo Hata

In a dream, Okuni dances and flirts with young male actors who resemble Nagoya Sanza.

Dream Sanzas: Teruko Nakayama, Sachiko Tsuruoka, Yuko Aoki

Longing for her lost love Nagoya Sanza, Okuni dances in male costume.

A duet between Okuni in male costume and Densuke in female costume.

Okuni: Michiyo Hata
Densuke: Yasushige Tsuruoka

A rumor spreads that Nagoya Sanza has been killed in a fight, and Okuni is wracked with grief. In a dream, he comes to her in the guise of a townsman, having abandoned his samurai status, and she is overjoyed.

Okuni: Michiyo Hata
Nagoya Sanza: Tokusaburo Arashi

The members of Okuni's troupe rejoice at a gift of many luxurious robes from Nagoya Sanza.

Okuni is performing in Kyoto in spring, at the height of the season of the cherry blossoms, when Nagoya Sanza, who she had thought dead, appears in the audience. His face remains covered, for he has returned from the dead to dance with Okuni, much to the delight of the audience.

Okuni dons the costume of the departed Nagoya Sanza to the tremendous response of her audience.

Okuni's troupe performs with growing popularity.

120 | CHAPTER FIVE

The classical style of Okuni's troupe (in the background) and Kikunokai's dance of the future interweave in an exciting finale to the work.

Nagoya Sanza, now a commoner, says that he will remain with Okuni forever as they create new dances and bring them to Asia, Europe, and America.

THE WORKS OF KIKUNOKAI | 121

AI NO HITO
(Indigo Woman)

Written and directed
by Haruo Misumi
Choreography by
Michiyo Hata
Music by Misao Suzuki

Ai no Hito is set in the turbulent Meiji Period, when Japan opened up to the world after centuries of isolation. Its heroine is a geisha, Matsuba, a master of the shamisen and a famous singer in the Pontocho geisha district of Kyoto. Her father was a samurai, but both he and her mother were killed when she was very young. Over the years, the loss has turned her into a bitter, rebellious woman.

RIGHT
Matsuba has gotten herself in trouble by singing a satirical song to a samurai patron, but a wealthy indigo merchant *(ai shonin)* from Tokushima rescues her from her dilemma. He is attracted to her spirit and pluck and asks her to return with him to Tokushima.

Matsuba as geisha:
Michiyo Hata
Indigo Merchant:
Hatsuo Ito

Matsuba dances with Densuke.

Matsuba: Michiyo Hata
Densuke: Satoshi Hara

Sparks of rivalry fly when geisha in the gay quarters of Tokushima show off the kimono they will wear at an upcoming festival.

After many dramatic trials and tribulations on Tokushima, Matsuba is transformed by love and a new appreciation of human kindness.

Toramatsu: Shingo Horii
Matsuba: Michiyo Hata

NIPPON
O-DORI
(Nippon Boulevard)

Written and directed by Haruo Misumi
Choreography by Michiyo Hata
Music by Misao Suzuki

Kiku: Michiyo Hata
Kamekichi: Nagamitsu Satake
Renzo: Satoshi Hara
Fusazo: Yasushige Tsuruoka

Nippon O-Dori is set in Yokohama in the Edo period. With the signing of a treaty with the United States in 1858, the port of Yokohama was opened and some hundred families had to be evacuated for the port's construction. The father and fiancée of the heroine, Kiku, were executed years ago by the Japanese feudal government, and she lives on the edge of poverty. Faced with dislocation, she leaves her younger sister Kohana with relatives and goes with her friend Tomi to become a dancer at the Yamatoro, a theater of song and dance.

Not only Japanese but foreigners also frequent the Yamatoro. The high official Smith has designs on Tomi, and a Japanese official threatens that he will close Yamatoro if she refuses Smith's advances. Kiku is enraged when she learns that this Japanese official was responsible for the execution of her beloved. Protesting Tomi's abuse by the high officials, Kiku kills herself.

RIGHT, BELOW
The villagers are forced to leave their homes by the government, but three young men, Fusazo, Kamekichi, and Renzo vow that one day they will return.

In the second part of the dance, Kiku's younger sister Kohana returns to their old home. As she gazes at the sea, filled with nostalgia, she discovers two men doing the same: Sakichi, who once ran the Yamatoro, and the Western-style composer Renzo.

After Kiku killed herself, Sakichi closed the Yamatoro and became a wanderer, but, unable to forget Kiku, he has returned. Renzo, too, is unable to forget his home town and, after seeing Kohana by the shore, the exact image of Kiku, decides with Sakichi to open another theater.

Kohana: Michiyo Hata
Renzo: Satoshi Hara
Sakichi: Shingo Horii

The name of the new theater is the Nihonza. The curtain goes up on opening day, and the entire ensemble dances with great enthusiasm.

KOTO SAIJIKI
(A Record of the Four Seasons in the Ancient Capital)

Choreography by Michiyo Hata

LEFT, ABOVE
Young apprentice geishas, still innocent in the flush of youth, dance.

LEFT, BELOW
Geisha dancing in beautiful autumn colors.

Geisha: Sachiko Tsuruoka

ABOVE
Koto Saijiki (A Record of the Four Seasons in the Ancient Capital) describes the four seasons of Kyoto by the different flowers in bloom.

Flower seller: Rika Miyazawa

OPPOSITE
Kyoto has preserved ancient customs. For the geisha of the Gion quarter, the the preparation for the coming new year begins on December 13, when they bring rice cakes to their teachers of dance and music and to their senior geisha to show their gratitude.

Maiko: Sayuri Yasue, Asuka Tsuchiya

The winters in Kyoto are cold. Popular actors perform in a special performance called the *kaomise* at the historical Minamiza Kabuki Theater every December. Here they are presenting a scene from *Shakkyo* (The Stone Bridge), a frequent *kaomise* offering.

The beautiful four seasons of Kyoto repeat in an endless cycle of death and rebirth.

OIWAKE NO HITO
(Woman at the Crossroads)

Written and directed by Haruo Misumi
Choreography by Michiyo Hata
Music by Misao Suzuki
Set and costume design by Yusuke Misumi

Miya Hanayama: Michiyo Hata
Reijiro Teshima: Shingo Horii
Saki: Kasumi Kimura
Heizo Tamiya: Norio Takei
Fusako Tamiya: Asuka Tsuchiya

Oiwake no Hito is a paean to love based on the famous song *Esashi Oiwake,* or "Esashi Crossroads," set in the harbor town of Esashi on the northernmost island of Hokkaido.

RIGHT, ABOVE
Esashi once flourished as a herring fishing ground, but as the herring moved north, it declined. The other wealthy merchants have all departed, and only the widow Miya Hanayama keeps the town going. One day an old lover, Reijiro, appears and Miya is deeply shaken. When the time comes for Reijiro to return home, he asks Miya to leave Esashi with him. Deeply torn, Miya finds herself standing at a crossroads (*oiwake*) in her life; but realizing how the townpeople of Esashi depend upon her for their living, she decides to stay.

RIGHT, BELOW
The two young heirs to an old family business in Tokyo, Heizo and his bride Fusako, flee to Esashi. They have fallen into adversity and are prepared to die, but Saki, who works for Miya, stops them. To encourage Heizo and Fusako she sings *Esashi Oiwake* (Esashi Crossroads), the song that cheers the people during the town's severe winters.

KATCHA
IKANEKA
KONO
MICHI O
(Mother Won't You Go
This Way?)

Written and directed by
Haruo Misumi
Choreography by
Michiyo Hata
Music by Misao Suzuki

Sae Hatakeyama: Michiyo
Hata
Tomekichi: Satoshi Hara

Katcha Ikaneka Kono Michi o is set in the Tohoku region in 1934, during a terrible famine. The heroine Sae of the wealthy Hatakeyama clan, is to marry Tomekichi, who will be adopted into her family until the blood heir is old enough to succeed. On the day of their wedding a woman suddenly appears and leaves an infant and a measure of white rice before fleeing. The young couple adopt the child, name him Kensaku, and raise him as their own.

During a brief lunch break from their hard farm work, the villagers tell stories of how astonishingly kind and gentle Tomekichi is, and share many a laugh at his expense. As an outsider, Tomekichi feels very sad and lonely, but he gradually makes friends with the local young people. He teaches them a dance of his home town, *Oni Kenbai* (The Demon Sword Dance). He also teaches it to his wife Sae and their adopted child Kensaku.

KAZAMICHI
(The Path of the Wind)

Directed and set design
by Tetsuhiko Maeda
Choreography by Michiyo
Hata
Music by Nao Yamamoto

Kazamichi (The Path of the Wind) is a paean to the four seasons in Japan, celebrating the oneness of humanity and nature. Above, several male dancers try to cross a half-frozen stream, fighting against the cold, until the first rays of the spring sun melt the ice and the stream flows freely. Below, the spirits of spring appear, dancing in the wind as lightly as dandelion seeds floating on the breeze.

With the arrival of the new year, people set out on a journey toward the light of hope.

ABOVE
Young women dance with glee at the arrival of spring.

LEFT
Dancing joyfully like the golden heads of rice of the rich autumn harvest.

THE WORKS OF KIKUNOKAI

Michiyo Hata dances through the star-filled night sky as the spirit of the moon.

IWAI DAIKO
(Celebratory Drumming)

The *taiko* drum is the beat of life, a language all its own, which can express the joy of being alive as well as anger at evil.

HOKKAI TAIRYO BUSHI
(Hokkai Fisherman's Song)

In this dance, set on Hokkaido, Japan's northernmost island, a fishing boat with a full catch has returned to harbor and a joyous celebration ensues.

ARASHI NO JOKYOKU
(Storm Overture)

Fishermen set out to sea only to run into a fierce storm. They work together to overcome the raging waves and winds and return safely to harbor.

The contrast of the beautiful movements of the female dancers, depicting the waves with lengths of cloth, and the vigorous movements of the male dancers riding the waves is striking against the darkness.

THE WORKS OF KIKUNOKAI | 143

ECCHU OWARA BUSHI

Each year on the night of a summer festival, a well-bred young woman, discouraged from dancing because it was considered disreputable, stands quietly near her doorway longing to see the parade of dancers. Wishing she could join them but hesitant to leave home, she dances by herself until, carried away by her feelings, she finally chases after the dancers.

Young woman: Michiyo Hata

OYAMA-BAYASHI
(Folk Song of Akita)

This dance is set at the harvest festival, a time of joy and release for the hardworking farmers. Young and old gather for music, singing and dancing. The dance of the young women, wearing bright, beautiful costumes, is the center of attention.

TSUCHIGUMO
(The Giant Spider)

The festival is over and everyone goes home. Night falls, and the figures on the festival floats come to life. The giant spider casts his web to catch his enemies.

Spider: Hideharu Takeda

SHOGORO ODORI
(Shogoro's Dance)

Shogoro Odori is a dance from Ibusuki in Kyushu. It is said to have originated from an incident in which a retainer, having received a present from his lord, in his extreme happiness put on his wife's brightly colored kimono and danced happily in it.

KASA ODORI
(Parasol Dance)

In the old days *Kasa Odori* was performed as a rain dance in Tottori Prefecture, but it eventually turned into a dance in which the young men of the village showed their mettle, and it survives to this day as a staple of the folk repertory.

KAGOSHIMA SUMOTORI BUSHI
(Song of Sumo at Kagoshima)

A comical dance imitating sumo wrestlers.

Wrestlers: Nagamitsu Satake, Yasushige Tsuruoka

ONI KENBAI
(The Demon Sword Dance)

Oni Kenbai is one of Japan's most dynamic folk dances. The demon wears a mask and carries a fan and a sword. A protective deity, he stamps forcefully on the ground to drive away the evils and calamities that threaten us.

OPPOSITE
Oni Kenbai performed in Komoro City, Nagano Prefecture. The lead dancer wears a white mask.

Dancer: Shigeru Edaki

AWA ODORI
(Awa Dance)

Women dance gracefully and men powerfully to the happy rhythms of the south. As the melody shifts, the dancers' movements grow more restrained, demonstrating subtle variations.

This happy and varied dance is popular throughout Japan.

The male dancers tuck up their kimono and dance in a half-stooped position. The female dancers wear hats and dance on the tips of their wooden clogs.

IWATE-KEN YANAGAWA KANATSURYU SHISHI ODORI
(Yanagawa Deer Dance)

This is a dance for eight male dancers performed for a wide range of purposes: as thanks for a good harvest, as a prayer for rain, to drive away crop pests, and to honor the ancestors. The dance is directed by the song of the lead dancer and the rhythms of the *taiko*.

AHOBAYASHI
(Drum Performance)

"Fools dance and fools watch; better a dancing fool than a watching fool!" The *taiko* drummers pound out a liberating rhythm for this joyful dance.

OTOMEDAKE
(Bamboo Maiden)

The spirit of the young bamboo longs for an escape from her proscribed realm.

ABOVE
Under the all-embracing light of the moon, she dreams of falling in love with someone in the outside world and a life of freedom.

Michiyo Hata poses as the spirit in a bamboo forest owned by the Usui family, Saga, Kyoto.

Chronology

Kikunokai is dedicated to the correct transmission of the tradition of Japanese dance and its continued growth and development. Founded by Michiyo Hata in 1972, it is based firmly on the fundamentals of classical Japanese dance, and also studies the folk dance traditions of all regions in Japan, aiming at enriching the hearts of its audiences by creating a new folk or people's dance art.

Kiku is the Japanese word for "chrysanthemum," a flower symbolic of Japanese culture. Hata chose this name to represent the flowering of each individual's full potential through the process of mastering the art of dance, and also because she wanted to create emotionally moving dances with all the harmony and elegance that beautiful flower suggests.

In the twenty-eight years since its founding, Kikunokai has created and performed numerous new works, engaged actively in cultural exchange with many other nations, and worked to nurture young dance talent while carrying out research on regional folk traditions and preserving their source materials. It has won many awards and honors, and has a high reputation.

1972
April 1: Kikunokai founded

1973
January: Debut performance, *Kojika yo Odore* and *Furusato Bayashi*; formation of the Kojika Group (boys' group)
April: Performances in India and Singapore
November: Performance in Guam

1974
October: Performance of the dance-drama *Okesa Umi o Yuku*

1975
February: Performance in France; formation of Himawari Group (girls' group)

1976
November: Performance of the dance-drama *Katcha Ikaneka Kono Michi o* in the Culture Festival sponsored by the Agency for Cultural Affairs of Japan, and wins the Prize for Outstanding Artistry

1977
February: Performance in France

1978
October: Performance of dance-drama *Ai no Hito*

1979
June: Performance in Bangkok, Thailand

1980
Formation of the young men's Wakajishi Group
May: Performance of *Shioakari* at Hakuhinkan, Tokyo
September: First performance of Wakajishi Group
December: Performances of *Chidori no Kyoku* and dance-drama *Wakaki Onitachi no Sanka*

1981
June: European tour
October: Performance of *Bashamichi no Hitobito* at Hibiya Public Hall, Tokyo
November: Performance in Taiwan

1982
April: Celebration of the 10th anniversary of the founding of Kikunokai; formation of Kikunokai Tomo no Kai (Kikunokai support group)
December: Performance of *Shibuki o Agete Fune o Dase!*

1983
Performance of *Akatsuki no Shima ni Odoru*
December: Participation in the first SGI Hong Kong Culture Festival

1984
February: Performance at ceremonies for the establishment of the Kingdom of Brunei, sponsored by the Japan Foundation
April: Kikunokai Folk Song Festival

1985
February: Tour of the Middle East, sponsored by the Japan Foundation
April: Establishment of the classical dance study group Kikushunju
September: Debut performance of *Komai no Michi*

1986
May: Performance of *Katcha Ikaneka Kono Michi o*
July: Receives official commendation from the Ministry of Foreign Affairs of Japan for international exchange achievement
September: Performance at the Japan-China Friendship Music Festival
December: Performance in Taiwan

1987
May: 15th anniversary performance, *Katcha Ikaneka Kono Michi o*

1988
January-February: Performances in Kuala Lumpur and Penang, Malaysia; formation of the Tenmai Group
April: Performance in Australia

1989
First performances for elementary school students begin, *Nihon no Kokoro o Odoru*
May: Performances of *Furusato Bayashi* and other works

1990
February: Performances in Singapore
April: Performance at the International Garden and Greenery Exposition, Osaka
May: Choreography for and performance in Akira Kurosawa's Oscar-winning film *Yume (Dreams)*
June: Performance of *Kazamichi* at the Kyurian Theater
October: Performance with Min-on Concert Association of *Odori Fudoki*, *Tsuri Onna*, and *Kazamichi*

1991
June: Performances in Hawaii and Okinawa
November: Performance at the Japan Festival '91 in Great Britain
December: Performance of *Miko no Tsuka* in the Creative Dance Exhibition

1992
May: Performance for Japan Festival '91 in Great Britain sponsored by Min-on Concert Association, Shibuya Public Concert Hall; 20th anniversary performance of the dance-drama *Ai no Hito*

1993
14th Matsuo Arts Prize Special Award for Dance given to Michiyo Hata and Kikunokai
November: Performances of *Nippon no Odori*, *Wakaki Onitachi no Sanka*, and other works

1994
March: Completion of the Kikunokai Dance Studio and performance of dance-drama *Okuni Kabuki*
June: Performance of *Hisho* at the 12th World Youth Peace and Culture Festival at the Liric Theater, Milan
August: Performance in Aizu of *Umi Haruka Nippon o Odoru* and other works
November: Performance in Tokyo of the dance-drama *Okuni Kabuki*

1995
August: Performance of *Okuni Kabuki* at Minamiza, Kyoto
November: Performance of *Ai no Hito* in Tokyo

1996
September: Performance of dance-drama *Nippon O-Dori*
November: Performance of *Nihon Buyo no Saiten* at the Min-on Concert Association, Nepal Cultural Exchange Festival, Katmandu City International Convention Center

1997
April: First and third prizes (for *Shakkyo* and *Shima no Senzai*, respectively) in the "Japanese Dance Division" of the Tokyo Shimbun 54th Japan Nationwide Dance Competition
May: Opening of the Kikunokai Kyoto Yase Training Center
October: Performance in New Delhi as part of the Japan-India Friendship and Culture Festival celebrating the 50th anniversary of Indian independence
November: Performances of *Katcha Ikaneka Kono Michi o*, *Kanbotan*, *Take* (Music: Ogiebushi)

1998
April: First, second, and third prizes (for *Shiokumi*, *Yoshinoyama*, and *Oborozuki*, respectively) in the "Japanese Dance Division" of the Tokyo Shimbun 55th Japan Nationwide Dance Competition
July: Performance of *Yuya* in the 50th anniversary celebrations of the founding of the Onoe School, at the Shimbashi Embujo Theater
September: Performance of *Setsugekka ni Mau, Part 1* sponsored by the Arakawa Ward Regional Promotion Association
November: Performances of *Kuroshio*, *Otomedake*, *Migawari Zazen*, *Furusato no Kokoro ni Mau*

1999
April: First, second, and third prizes (for *Ume no Sakae*, *Kiku*, and *Saginusume*, respectively) in the "Japanese Dance Division" of the Tokyo Shimbun 56th Japan Nationwide Dance Competition
May: Satsukikai Concert for the education of young dancers; performance of *Ganoiwai*, *Kamuro*, *Fujimusume*, *Tamausagi*, and *Furusato Bayashi* by the professional performers' group of Kikunokai
September: Performance of *Nippon no Odori* jointly by Arakawa Ward Local Promotion Association
October: Performance at Kyung Hee University, Seoul, to commemorate the completion of the Kyung Hee University Auditorium; Performance of *Nippon no Odori*, *Fuji Musume*, *Shakkyo*, *Migawari Zazen*, and *Shiki ni Mau* sponsored by Chiba Prefecture Cultural Promotion Association; Performance of the dance-drama *Katcha Ikaneka Kono Michi o* at Nakano Zero Hall
December: Performance of dance-drama *Oiwake no Hito* at Shinjuku Bunka Center, Tokyo

2000
April: First and second prizes (for *Tomoyakko* and *Fujimusume*, respectively) in "Japanese Dance Division 1," and third prize in the "Japanese Dance Division 2" of the Tokyo Shimbun 57th Japan Nationwide Dance Competition; performance of dance-drama *Oiwake no Hito* at Yokohama Kannai Hall; performance of the dance-drama *Oiwake no Hito* at the Aoba no Mori Park Geijutsu Bunka Hall, Chiba, sponsored by Chiba Prefecture Cultural Promotion Association
May: Satsukikai Concert, performance of *Kotosaijiki*, *Umiharuka*, *Nippon o Odoru*
September: Performance of *Nippon no Odori* sponsored by the Arakawa Ward Local Promotion Association
December: Performances of dance-drama *Hakata Dontaku Monogatari* at Nihon Seinenkan Hall, Tokyo, and Hakataza, Hakata City

2001
March: U.S. Tour of "Nippon no Odori—Kikunokai Nihon no Kokoro o Odoru," supported by the Agency for Cultural Affairs of Japan and the Tokyo Metropolitan Foundation for History and Culture, performances of *Kazamichi*, *Otomedake*, and *Umiharuka Nippon o Odoru*, Kaye Playhouse, New York, and Japan America Theater, Los Angeles
June: publication of *Tradition and Creativity in Japanese Dance: The Works of Kikunokai*

The "weathermark" identifies this book as a production of Weatherhill, Inc., publisher of fine books on Asia and the Pacific. Editorial supervision: Jeff Hunter. Book and cover design: Mariana Canelo. Production supervision: Bill Rose. Printed in China. The typefaces used are Centaur and Gill Sans.